IT ONLY HURTS FOR . . .
A LIFETIME

The family ties that bind can
often unravel.

Jill Stone

A mother's search for solutions
that will touch the hearts and
minds of every reader.

To order additional copies of this book, contact:
Xlibris Corporation
1-888-795-4274
www.Xlibris.com
Orders@Xlibris.com
43795

DEDICATION

This book is dedicated to my husband Allen whose assistance and support was invaluable. It could not have been written without his considerable expertise as an author, broadcast journalist and advertising executive.

SPECIAL THANKS

To Richard Oakey, the talented creative specialist who contributed to the design of the book. Rich is the best of the best. He served with distinction as a colleague of my husband's during his years as an advertising executive.

The next time somebody asks me what I do, I will quote from an email I received.

"I'm a research associate in the field of child development and human relations."

Translation: I'M A MOM!

Is there any profession more demanding, more rewarding, or more worthy of commitment?

CONTENTS

INTRODUCTION

Life has its ups and downs. A time-worn cliché, but also an inescapable truth.

From the time I was born in an area of the Philadelphia suburbs known as the Main Line, I have enjoyed many exhilarating ups in combination with several punishing downs. But all along the way, I made every effort to avoid lapses in judgment and untoward behavior.

That is not to say that I am a perfect person. Who is? And who among us doesn't have regrets for the mistakes we've made?

However, in truth, I have tried my best to be a good wife, good mother and good grandmother.

Despite the fact that I am very private, with this book I am opening the door to my life. It is my hope that the manner in which I have met the challenges I faced and the attempts I made to free myself from anxiety might serve as guideposts for those coping with strained family relationships. That is the purpose of the book.

The stories herein are real but I have avoided the use of actual names to help guard the privacy of those involved.

I do not claim to be an oracle able to offer up magical pathways to a fuller life. Nor do I have the credentials of a behavioral professional. This book is not a scientific study or the result of scholarly research. It is a personal memoir, a chronicle of perceptions kindled by experience and observation. At the outset of each chapter, I have quoted from Webster as a clue to what's ahead.

Should you find something of value in what I have written, I will have been amply rewarded.

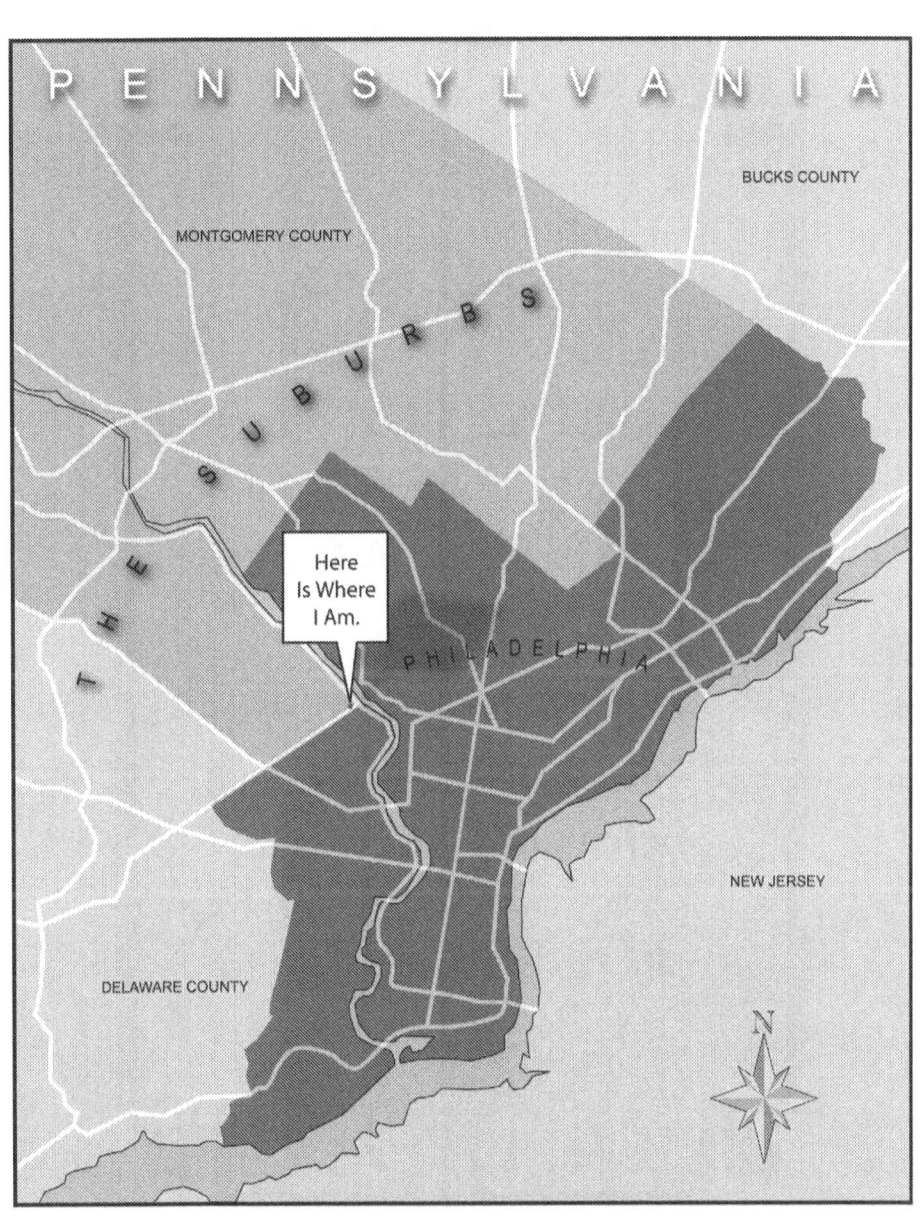

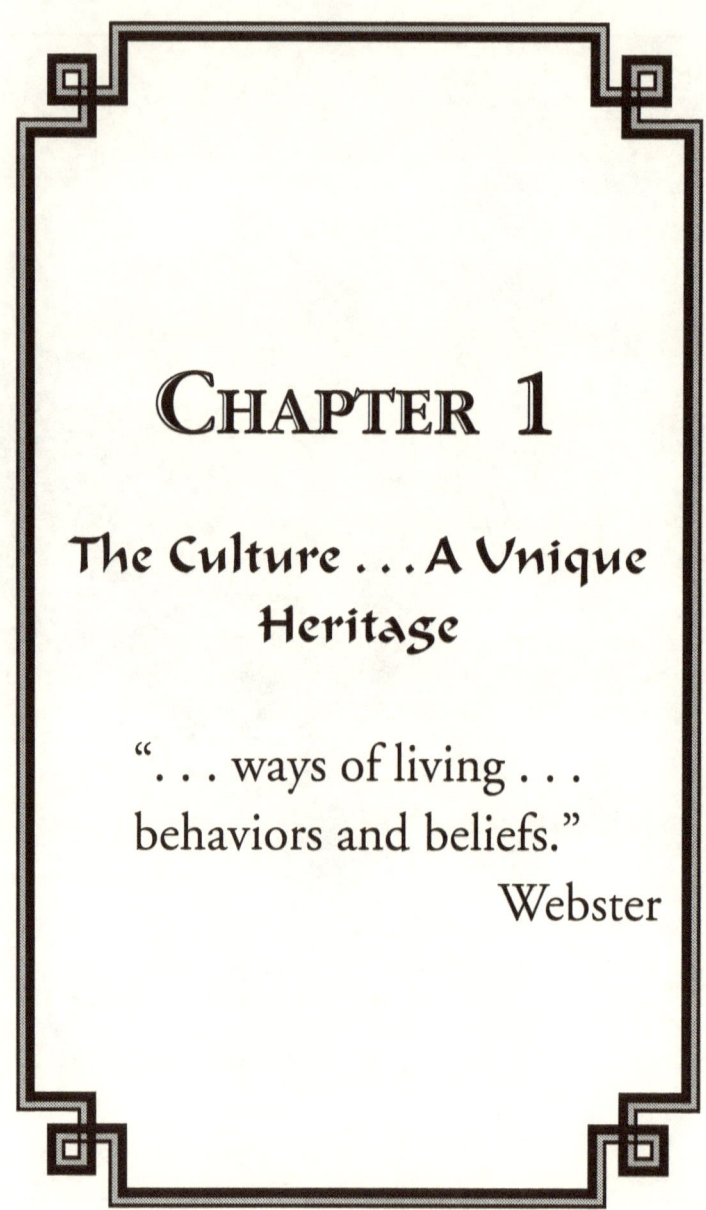

CHAPTER 1

The Culture . . . A Unique Heritage

". . . ways of living . . .
behaviors and beliefs."

Webster

IN THIS FIRST chapter, I'd like to set the stage for what's coming in the book by offering a brief word picture of my background.

A large number of families who have settled in the counties surrounding Philadelphia trace their lineage to the city neighborhoods of their childhood. They have come to regard these breeding grounds as iconic signposts of the past.

To have been a native Philadelphian is a badge of honor they wear with pride.

These strong neighborhood identities have spawned lasting relationships that began in the city and persisted in the migration to the suburbs.

Interestingly, when those of us who share this heritage travel to far off places and someone asks where we are from, we're quick to say Philadelphia. But at home we think of ourselves, not any longer as Philadelphians, but as residents of the towns and villages that make up the suburban landscape.

As young parents, we were focused on doing the best for our children—teaching them the realities of life and inculcating the strengths to cope with those realities.

We were dedicated to preparing our sons and daughters to become productive members of society, so they too could enjoy the "American dream."

But, as many parents have learned, that road—although paved with the best intentions—can come up against unforeseen barriers, which has been the case in my own life.

My next chapter takes up one of the most devastating of those barriers.

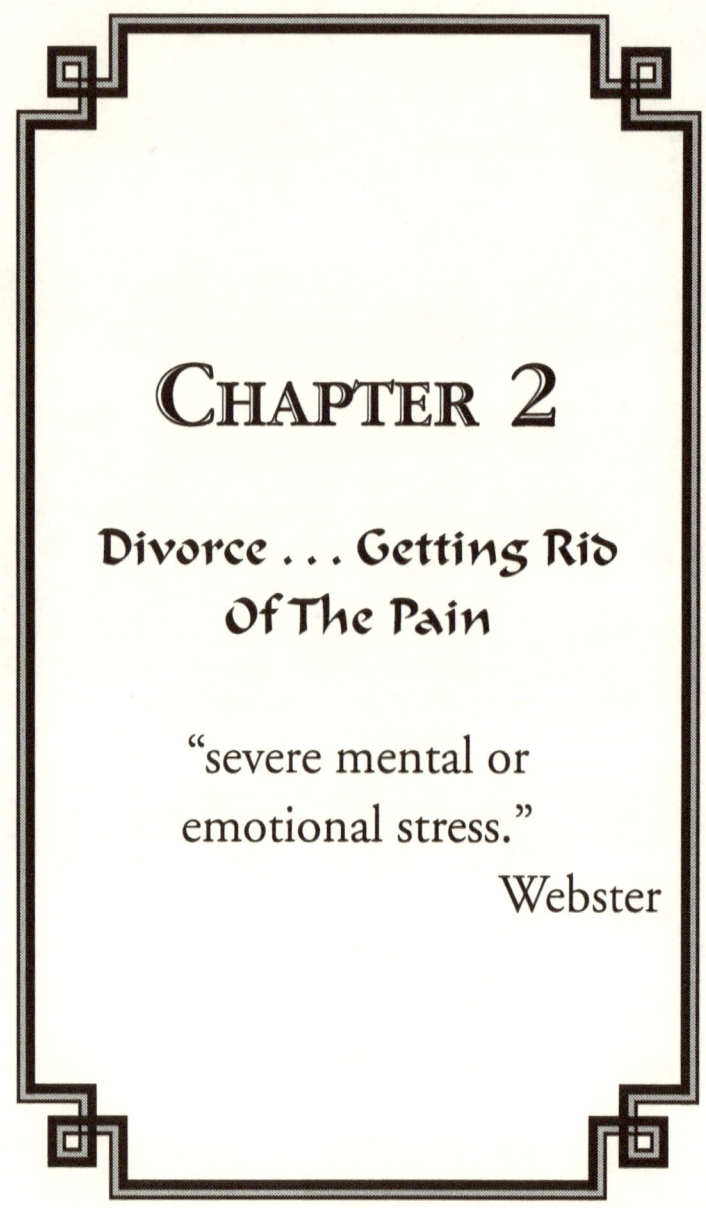

Chapter 2

Divorce . . . Getting Rid Of The Pain

"severe mental or
emotional stress."

Webster

I HAD ONLY been alive for a short 15 years when my parents were divorced. Among their circle of friends, divorce was not only shocking, it was embarrassing and even scandalous. Especially since my father was a well known Philadelphia industrialist and he and my mother were socially prominent. My sister, brother and I were humiliated, ashamed and traumatized. People were talking, gossiping and pointing fingers. Unlike now when divorce is a common occurrence virtually free of an irredeemable stigma.

Be that as it may, I became physically ill and, for protection, built a wall around myself so nothing or no one could hurt me or cause me more pain. If you have suffered through a like experience, my words at this point no doubt are dredging up bitter recollections.

As the divorce progressed, I remained with my mother in our large but empty house. My brother stayed with our father and my older sister finished college, married and moved on with her life. As for me, I sank into a pattern of feeling emotionally alone since my mother was totally devastated and spent her days behind the closed door to her room. Those years were a never-ending nightmare.

I vowed never to find myself at the precipice of divorce—a vow that was broken into pieces close to 40 years and three children later.

The lesson learned is never say never. And if you are no longer able to cope with the failure of your own marriage and frustrated at every bend in the road, by no means deny yourself the right to shuck off the ties that bind and rework your life. As my friend, psychologist and best selling author Judith Sills once said . . . if the horse is dead, get off.

To quote from *Necessary Losses*, authored by Washington Psychoanalytic research affiliate Judith Viorst: "Growth and change in mid-life may mean reworking, making peace with or putting an end to previous arrangements. But whichever approach we choose, life won't be the same."

And for me, it never was!

At the time of my divorce, our three children were grown. The youngest was already in college. They were all aware that their mother and father were nearing the abyss. My son and older daughter were quick to accept reality. They encouraged me to do the same and get on with my life. In contrast, my younger daughter was very angry with me. She was 15 years younger than her sister and 11 years younger than her brother. I really believe that to this day she blames me for breaking up the family. She has also rejected my present husband's many efforts to win her respect and affection. This rupture has spawned consequences that are devastating . . . particularly because there are grandchildren.

You know whereof I speak if you have endured a similar situation that has shredded your family life. I'll say more about this and offer some pointers on how I've dealt with it in a later chapter.

Meanwhile, I think you would agree if you have worked your way through the calamity of a divorce that even if both partners eventually find a better life—as I have—you fear you'll be penalized for the rest of your life. The lingering scars are imbedded in your being. And it's not easy to get rid of them . . . though you must never stop trying to do that, for the sake of your own health and well being in addition to your ability to enrich a second marriage.

How does it happen that children in the same family can be so different, one from the other?

My older daughter is my rock and redeemer. She is a one woman support group for me. I do not exaggerate when I refer to her as my guardian angel—always urging me to turn away from difficult and disappointing experiences. She has built an enviable career as a school system psychologist, is married to a talented lawyer and together, they have raised two beautiful children who cherish the time they spend with me. This is also true of my husband's children and grandchildren. His first wife died in 1985 and his two sons had the good grace to be pleased and accepting when their father met me and was able to start a new life.

Now you're asking . . . what about my son? To this point, I have mentioned him only briefly. He lives with his wife and my grandson in Southern California. He is a handsome macho type who checks in often with his mom, never forgets her birthday and opens his heart whenever I'm troubled and need a kind word.

I am very proud of his accomplishments as a commercial film director and businessman. Though that was not always the case due to the unimaginable events in his own life that could have marked the end of his ability to survive, not to speak of the despair it brought his parents. I thank God that his story had a happy ending, as you will read in the next chapter.

CHAPTER 3

Hitting Bottom . . .
Finding The Way Back

"An act that causes shame,
reproach or dishonor."

Webster

IT WAS AN agony I can never purge from my memory. It happened prior to the divorce. It was an offense that every parent fears and which continues to bring suffering to so many mothers and fathers.

I speak of the drug culture and how my own son, after falling victim to it, lost his freedom but—working against the odds—was able to reclaim his life and distinguish himself as a husband, father and career professional.

This is his story. And much of it in his own words. You will even feel, in reading his narrative, that you are with him, behind prison bars.

My son left our home after finishing high school. Out of the blue one day, he told us: "I got a ride to California. Solong!"

We always made it clear to our kids that we would provide for their education. When our son turned his back on college, he knew that meant he was on his own. So he walked out the door with nothing more than the clothes he was wearing. He ended up living in a commune at Berkeley with musicians, hippies and drug smugglers. He couldn't play a guitar so he got in with the drug smugglers—and that led to his arrest.

The following is my son's own account of his journey from Hell to the road back. An ordeal that would change his life forever. He calls it . . .

One Lucky Kid

So there I was in the San Francisco County Jail, probably ranked 2 or 3 among the worst county jails in our country. I was 25 years old, 5 foot 11 inches and damn cute according to my many girl friends. Even though I had been well provided by my family, I found myself in a bunch of trouble.

It was 1985 and I was selling kilos of cocaine to a large and brutally mean organization which, after months of investigation, was nailed—taking little old me with them. Scared does not do justice to my condition. Terrified and numb is a more apt description.

Entering the county jail handcuffed, with my head down to avoid my face being splattered across the 6'oclock news, I was led past each cell by a hulking guard whose expression seemed to exude hate from every pore. The crowded jailhouse cells housed vicious looking humans staring at me like I was a walking pork chop, probably hoping I would be put in their cells so they would have fresh meat to devour.

There was an eerie quiet which I feared was the calm before the storm. How long would it take for the carnivores to begin working on me? How long would I be removed from society? If I were to believe my lawyers, it could be up to 8 years with no time off for good behavior.

From behind the bars of a cell, I hear "hey, poot im in here." Suddenly, in that cell, I see a sad, smiling face, his finger pointing to the cell across from his. I recognize Marteen, my old heroin connection. Oh, I forgot to mention that I had developed a nasty heroin habit which I managed to kick 8 months before I was arrested. Marteen said nothing more until I was in the cell and the guard walked away. He then went to the back of his cell, returned to the front with a book in hand, bent down and slid the book across the floor from his cell to mine.

I opened the book to find a tiny envelope containing heroin and three joints. I kept the joints and slid the book back to Marteen with the heroin still in there. He looked at me *confused. I told him I don't do heroin any more.*

He said . . . "wow, you were a wild boy. I never thought you could stop. Good for you. I'm 50 years old and can't quit." Marteen, shaking his head, disappeared to the back of his cell. Every guard that worked that cellblock was on his payroll. When I turned to face my cellmates, most of them stared at me, trying to figure out how I rated a cell across from this powerful man and was given something from him within seconds of arriving. It was everyone's dream in there that they too could get something from Marteen since he was the man dealing the dope.

I sat on my bed, contemplating my fate and realizing thank God that I was not, at that point, in any physical danger.

Holding the three joints I kept from Marteen, I stared into space with a million thoughts racing through my head. Cutting through the stillness, I heard . . . "you gonna smoke that yourself or what?" To which I said, "I guess not." A cellmate they called Ham, in for double murder, rolled out toilet paper on the floor, painted *the paper with deodorant, wrapped the paper around his fist, took it off his hand, placed it near the front of our cell, lit a cigarette and before he blew out the match, lit the toilet paper. It was a prisoner's version of incense.*

Ham lit a joint and waited for me to do the same. I looked around the cell and thought what a ride! I'm in a ton of trouble but felt like one lucky kid. Marteen was keeping an eye on me. As a result, everyone else was treating me like a prince. Except a guy nearby who was a member of SLA, the group that allegedly kidnapped Patty Hearst. He began ranting at me, even threatened to kill me. It was starting to scare me and just when it threatened to overwhelm me, Marteen shouted . . . "Lucky, shut him the f up. Lucky was 6 feet five and 250 pounds. He would do anything Marteen asked, rather than risk a cutoff of his heroin supply.

Lucky, in the same cell as this guy, walks over to him and slams his face against the bars. That took care of it. He never threatened me again.

As if that wasn't enough good luck, another feather in my cap appeared *to enhance my status with my fellow inmates. One of my many lawyers had a connection with the chief of police who made it possible to have a ceremonial meal delivered to me at the end of a Yom Kippur fast. Between Marteen and the meal, everyone thought I was one powerful kid.*

It wasn't long before my son's luck ran out. The day of infamy came as he faced an uncompromising federal judge who ruled out rehabilitation as unworkable for drug users and pushers. Stiff sentences, the judge declared, are warnings that those who deal in the drug trade do so at their own peril.

He banged down his gavel—15 YEARS in Boron, the federal minimum security lockup at Barstow, California. Shocked into a state of near collapse, my husband and I received a measure of relief 3 and ½ years later when my son's attorney managed to get the sentence reduced to 4 years.

During those painful years, my husband and I either visited our son together or separately. Boron was both reality and unreality. We left our belongings in the car, not being allowed to take anything in. We sat on chairs in a large room waiting for our son to be brought in. The first time I saw him in that setting, my eyes filled with tears. My husband and I took care not to be judgmental during those visits. We were loving and supportive from beginning to end. For the most part, he seemed resolute in accepting his punishment. As you can imagine, it was so hard to leave him every time.

We appreciated the fact that several of our friends as well as his maintained contact with him—remaining loyal and supportive throughout the entire ordeal.

Ironically, his incarceration was to be the making of our son. Tough and resilient, despite his frustration at being removed from society, he worked miracles while serving his time. He was living proof that rehabilitation can work . . . and he did it for himself.

Through a mentor, who made the arrangements, he took to the books and earned a degree from Antioch College. He did this without a typewriter, hand writing every paper and every report. He made sure to keep himself physically fit and emotionally controlled. He was known as an accomplished athlete and became the star of the prison baseball team.

To this day, I hesitate to think what might have happened to him if he had not been caught and put away.

When I look at my son today, I see a man who has carved out an enviable place in his world, who is married to a California beauty, is devoted to his own son, to his entire family and to the best that life has to offer. I shudder to think that it could have been otherwise.

If you are fighting your way out of a similar horror, keep in mind that hope springs eternal, as it is said, and that rehabilitation can work.

I know because I got my son back and what more can a mother ask.

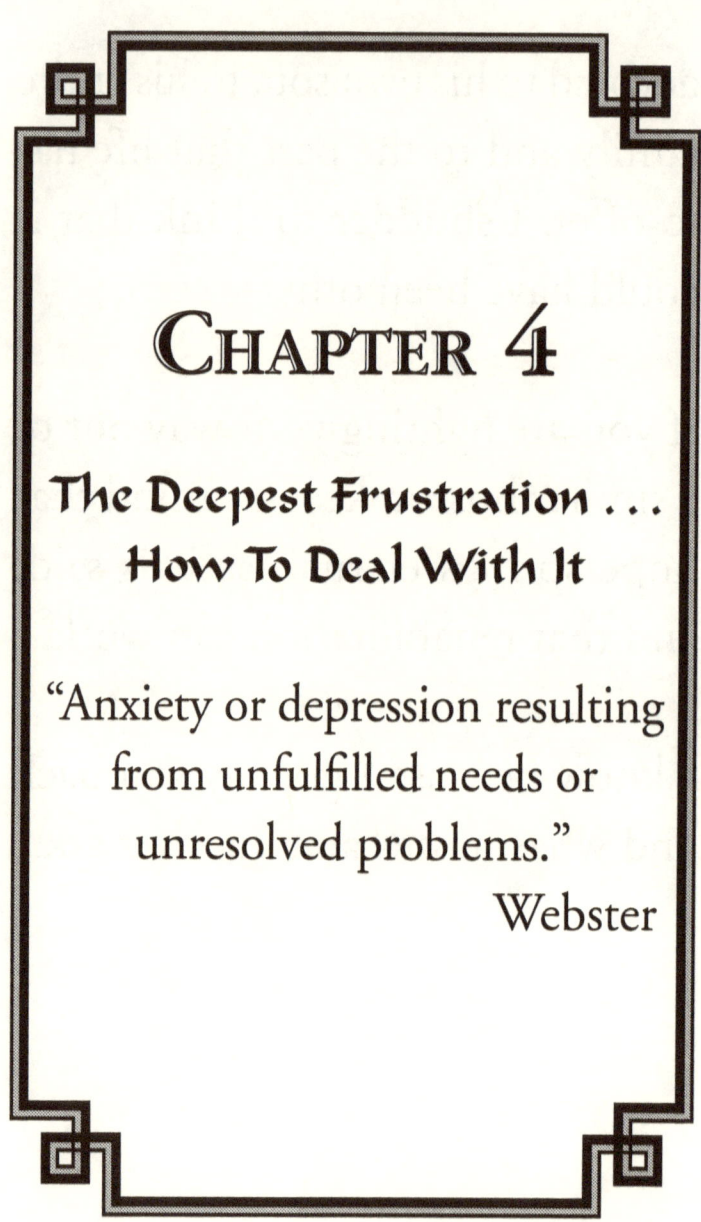

CHAPTER 4

The Deepest Frustration ...
How To Deal With It

"Anxiety or depression resulting
from unfulfilled needs or
unresolved problems."

Webster

THOSE OF US who have brought children into the world understand that parenting is not a science. It is an art—a combination of sensitivity, sacrifice, intuition, pure luck, the strength to roll with the punches and above all . . . unconditional love.

In her book *Motherhood, The Second Oldest Profession,* the late humorist Erma Bombeck hit the nail on the head when she wrote: "No mother is all good or all bad, all laughing or all serious, all loving or all angry." She goes on to characterize Motherhood as "the biggest on-the-job training program in existence."

The writings of Judith Wallerstein, the noted psychologist and researcher who spent 24 years studying the effects of divorce on children, helped me understand my own situation. Her most significant finding was that the impact of divorce on children is not short term or transient. It is long lasting, profound and cumulative. She says in her book, *The Unexpected Legacy Of Divorce*, that the greatest effect does not occur until children grow into their twenties and thirties.

That is borne out by what I have gone through with my younger daughter. But before I go on, let me say right here that she is an accomplished and talented mother in her own right. She has many friends and is living the good life, for which I am genuinely pleased.

Certainly there are lots of loving kids devoted to their parents and forever thankful for their teachings. Then there are those such as my daughter who hold their parents responsible for events and actions that have left them embittered and estranged—often unable to function as well-balanced mature adults.

To be sure, there are those cases where parents *are* to blame for the excesses of their children. In that regard, there's no question that the dislocations and confrontations that marked my marriage plus the upset caused by the divorce engendered a deep resentment in my younger daughter.

So how come my older daughter and son, though impacted by the divorce, were able to take it in stride and continue to offer their mom unending attention and devotion?

If I could answer that question, perhaps it would be easier for me to accept what is now occurring— not only to me but I'm sure to others who read this book and find common ground in their own lives.

Human decency is at stake in my relationship with my younger daughter. That is all I ask and want to give in return.

For example, I want her two children to know that they have a grandmother who loves them. That may never be possible because I feel I am not welcome in their home. I send them gifts every holiday and birthday. I write respectful letters to my daughter, expressing my need to visit with my grandchildren under any arrangement convenient for her.

I get no replies, with one exception.

She sent me a letter in which she said she didn't want to keep me from seeing her girls but did not have an answer for how to do it. She went on . . . "as more time passes, the more difficult it will be for you to be with the girls and that will hurt you. They should know you. You are their grandmother. I will try to figure this out for you in the way that is best for us all."

I wrote a return letter, thanking her for recognizing the hurt I feel and being willing to search for a solution. I told her . . . "it's very important to me and that will never change. I truly look forward to hearing from you when you feel able to open the door in some way."

As of the printing of this book, she had not responded.

In contrast, my new husband's granddaughter sent me the book *Grandmothers Are Like Snowflakes . . . No Two Are Alike*, authored by Janet Lanese. In it, this darling child wrote these words to me: "I wanted to let you know how much you mean to me. I'm so lucky to have you in my life. I love you more than all the candy in the world."

What I wouldn't give to hear the same thing from the two grandchildren who are not allowed to know me—and I'll never give up the hope that some day, we will become a family again.

What is the wisdom I can offer if you are in conflict with a son or daughter who mars your life with misery? First, take care that the stress does not damage your health. Get your doctor's advice if you feel you are running out of steam in trying to cope with the situation and need help. If there's anyone in your family whose good offices you can use to seek remedies, that may be worth a try. And beyond all else, don't freak out unless there's a reason.

If there are grandchildren involved, don't give up on trying to visit with them. But if that reaches a point of no return, you may have to back off and trust that one day, there will be light at the end of the tunnel.

When my daughter's two children grow up, it is inevitable that they will discover they have a grandmother who they vaguely remember and want to know where she is and why she hasn't come to see them.

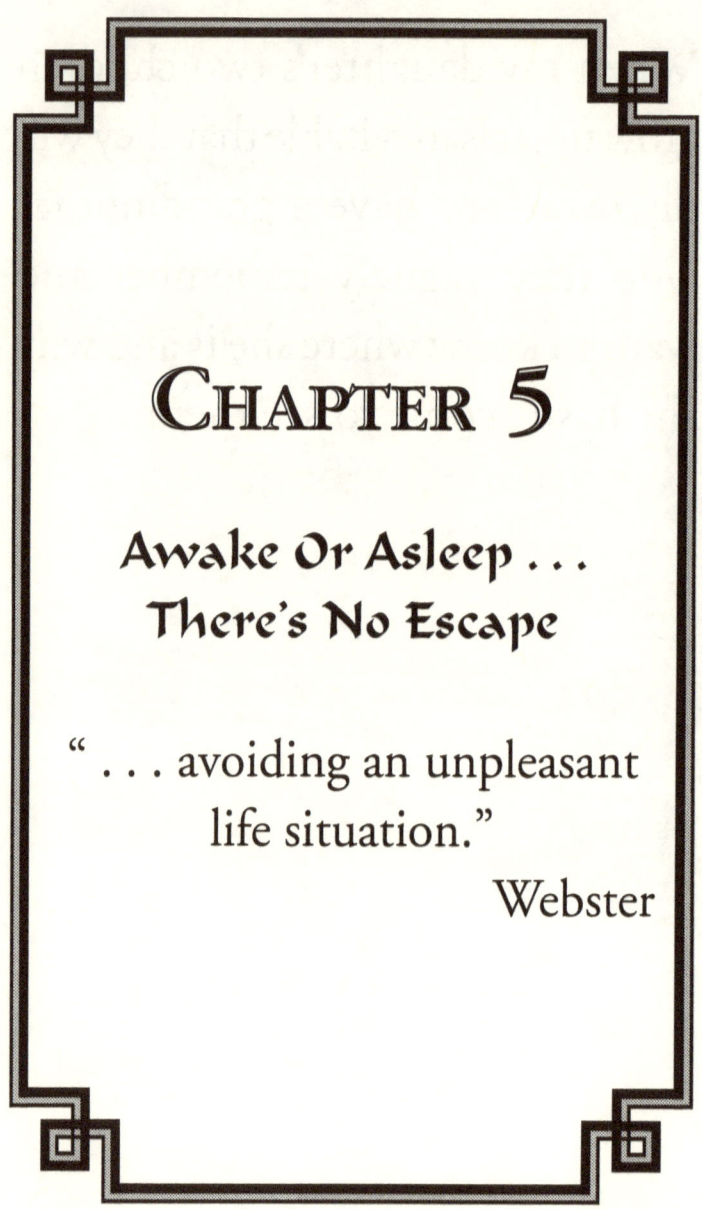

CHAPTER 5

Awake Or Asleep . . . There's No Escape

" . . . avoiding an unpleasant life situation."

Webster

IT ISN'T ENOUGH that the behavior of my daughter is in my thoughts virtually every waking hour, it has penetrated my subconscious—turning dreams into nightmares. In an effort to banish these torturous visions, I try to think positive about all the good things in my life. Easier said than done.

I envy my husband who claims he dreams in color. Undoubtedly because most of his life has been a halcyon journey.

He is a real Sir Galahad in helping me tolerate my daughter's hurtful behavior. I wish I could believe him when he says . . . *this too shall pass*. If only he could invade my dreams and do away with the demons.

Sigmund Freud believed that dreams are the road maps leading to where hidden feelings are stored. Scholars who study dreams tell us they can sometimes be helpful and liberating. In my case the images, thoughts and emotions that passed through my unconscious mind were anything but.

One recurring dream went on for a prolonged period of time. I saw myself running after a child but never being able to reach her. It was an obvious expression of the reality that my daughter was shutting me out of her life.

There are many variations of this disturbing vision. Often they are surreal to the point that I can't interpret their meaning, except that they are evidence of my troubled mind. The good news is that these upsetting nightmares, although not totally gone, are beginning to fade— perhaps indicating that I am starting to accept an unfortunate reality.

In attempting to do this, I tell myself:

Don't make the mistake of spending your waking hours dwelling on things you can't do anything about. It will only prolong the suffering.

Instead of feeling sorry for yourself, pull out all the stops in an effort to put a positive spin on your life.

Accept what you have to accept, hoping that time will bring changes but understand that it may not.

Because, according to Judith Viorst in her book *Necessary Losses*, "we know that reality cannot provide us with special treatment or absolute control."

I hope that some of this wisdom might give you sustenance if you're attempting some family problem solving of your own.

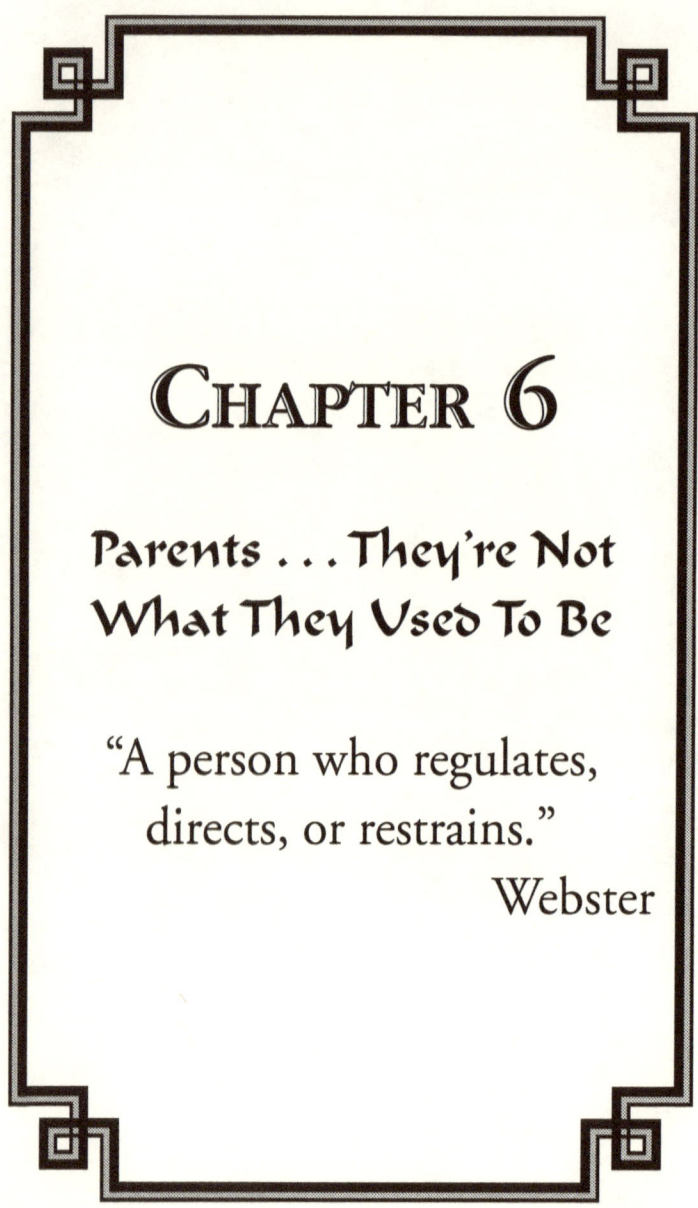

CHAPTER 6

Parents . . . They're Not What They Used To Be

"A person who regulates, directs, or restrains."

Webster

THAT'S WHAT THEY used to be. Maybe some still are. But in too many cases, peer groups have replaced parents as the arbiters of their children's behavior. Simply stated, parents don't count. Peer groups do. Is that happening in your family?

There was a time when parental control and reverence for the family were the most influential components in the health of our society. That seems to be breaking down, under the corrupting influences that cause many children to ignore the guidance of their parents . . . resulting in a profound affect on moral, ethical and emotional standards.

The problem I'm having with my daughter, though shameful, does not approach behavior of this magnitude and no doubt pales by comparison to what many parents are living through with their children. Why is this so? Why is there an increasing absence of strengths and disciplines on the part of many young people? Why are parents not what they used to be?

My husband has an interesting theory. It is by no means the whole answer but he feels it's worth considering as one element in the complex sociological equation facing parents today. At the same time, it should be recognized that there are those youngsters who travel the right road and make the right decisions—irrespective of what others among their peers are doing.

His perspective is drawn from growing up in the Depression. Most young people of that time had no choice but to toe the mark in helping the family survive. They could expect no more than 10 cents for a Saturday movie, sometimes not even that. And if they strayed and broke the rules, they would have to answer to their parents.

So did they go off the deep end and rebel against parental control?

That would not work in those days. Their only alternative was to develop the strengths and disciplines necessary to accept life as it was. In that regard, according to my husband, the Depression was a great teacher in the way it built character into young people who learned to live in a gray world and make the best of it.

The result was that when these Depression children matured into adulthood, the tough lessons learned in childhood, as the country struggled against the economic malaise, remained central to their character.

The young people of today never had this advantage. They have not known deprivation and have been given every opportunity—except for those shut out of the country's prosperity, often disadvantaged by the educational system, un-nurtured by their families, and refused entry into the job market other than at the lowest and most demeaning levels. Fortunately that is beginning to change. But the bottom line is that today's "me generation" has not lived through a character-building event such as the Depression. So because many are lacking in the tools to deal with challenges and pressures, they are open to the line of least resistance and look for ways to feel good whether right or wrong.

My husband emphasizes that he sees this as just one of the reasons some are weak in resisting forbidden fruit or benefiting from parental guidance and control. So where do they turn to find a port in the storm? The peer group.

And that's why he feels that parents are not what they used to be.

The best advice is to know who your children are hanging out with. Then you'll have an inkling as to where they're heading. It also needs to be kept in mind that parental control must always be exercised with good judgments and good intentions. Positive influence and well-meaning advice is one thing. Excessive and unrelenting domination is something else.

CHAPTER 7

A Private Person ...
So Much For That

"Freedom from the intrusion
of others in one's private life."
Webster

IN THE INTRODUCTION to this book, I indicated that opening the door to my life as guidance to others faced with strained family relationships would be difficult.

However I felt the need to do it even though I was brought up not to talk about private things. Family matters especially were not to be shared with others. I was told— don't be a tell-tale.

I have learned, when catching up with what's going on in the lives of people I know, to avoid gossip . . . which Webster defines as: *idle talk or rumor, especially about the private affairs of others.* These exchanges can be given to exaggeration and alteration as they are "whispered down the lane."

Gossip can, in fact, have injurious tentacles and far-reaching consequences. There can be a backlash. You can be misquoted. Your comments when not meant to be shared could be repeated and resented. Gossip is okay when it's harmless banter. But it's not okay when it enters territory better banished from a conversation.

Don't insinuate yourself into other people's lives. It's tempting to be a do-gooder, but common sense dictates that you should stay out of where you don't belong. An unwanted intrusion into a private matter can exacerbate the situation and cause even more grief.

I have lived by these rules of privacy and, by so doing, have earned the trust of others—even as I have also been admonished for being too private.

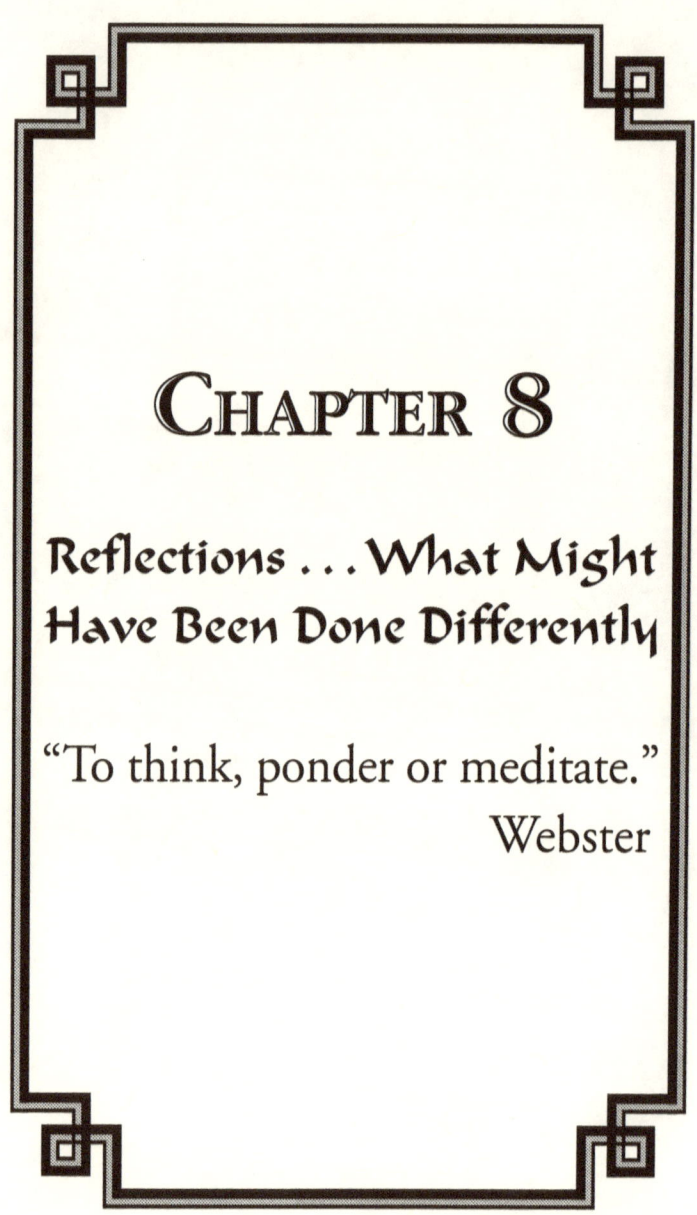

CHAPTER 8

Reflections ... What Might Have Been Done Differently

"To think, ponder or meditate."
Webster

MANY ARE THE books offering rules and guidelines for achieving a happy marriage and success as a parent. Yet, guaranteeing either is like searching for the Holy Grail.

As effective as we may be at dealing with both, it's likely that in retrospect, we might have some regrets and wish we had acted differently. With that in mind, lets go back and review the chapters to question what I could have done better.

The Divorce:

I wish I had taken more time to help my younger daughter deal with the trauma she suffered due to the divorce. I was selfish in paying too much attention to my own needs whereas I should have found ways to lessen the impact on her life.

Hitting Bottom:

My former husband and I should have been more involved in our son's interests and activities during his growing up years. Even during his adolescence, we failed to pick up on the directions he was taking.

The Deepest Frustration:

The only thing I can say here is that I wish there had been more opportunities to get closer to my daughter and understand more fully why she feels alienated.

No Escape:

I wish I had exercised more discipline in maintaining my sanity, rather than allowing the stresses and strains I was going through to invade my subconscious and affect my well being.

Peer Group Control:

Much as I counsel parents to know what their children's peer groups are up to, I regret not taking more time to keep tabs on my son's whereabouts, what he was doing and with who. If I had, perhaps the course of his life might have been different.

A Private Person:

Despite the fact that I have lived by the rules of privacy, I have made a couple of exceptions involving close friends who I believed would not violate my confidence. That was a mistake but it was also a lesson learned. So much for *would've, could've, should've*. It's water over the dam!

Epilogue

A New Husband, New Friends And A New Life

My life became very different following the divorce. To begin with, I had to walk away from 37 years of a marriage that eventually lost its luster. I knew that in order to carve out a new life, I had to open my eyes to a broader way of thinking.

My former husband had grown up with many friends from the time of childhood, through college, his days in the Air Force and into the years of our marriage. Between my friends and his friends, it was an inseparable group. Call it a clique. I was a kindergarten teacher for two years before the birth of our first child. By that time, most of our friends were not only married but having their own children.

We were bonded in good times— celebrating holidays, birthdays, anniversaries, Bar and Bat Mitzvahs.

Also in bad times. Two of the families lost children to illness, one to a tragic accident. We all came together, wrapping ourselves around them, trying our best to help ease their pain.

In reflection, perhaps the only negative was that we were all tied like an umbilical cord to each other's lives. At times, too much so. Especially the wives, which is understandable, recognizing that women need other women while men enjoy interaction and camaraderie with other men, but it is not a need.

After those 37 years, we were one of the first couples to divorce. Talk about change! Our group reacted with shock and disbelief. To this day, I don't think they have come to terms with it. For a time, they were supportive but it wasn't long before that changed. Meanwhile, I was having no problem finding places to go and things to do. There was an ample supply of those eager to help me do that.

After close to two years, I met my husband to be. He was not from

Philadelphia, not acquainted with *the group*, and very different from them. Though he tried, he was unable to relate to what they were all about and increasingly felt that he was an outsider.

When we married, I felt that a different direction was needed.

We added new friends we could admire and be comfortable with— people who are close to us but maintain their privacy and respect ours. However, I do want to say that many of my old friends remain dear to me and we do see each other, maybe not as frequently.

My life is more full, in part because my husband respects me as an individual, is proud of my accomplishments and loves having me at his side whenever it's important to make a favorable impression. He compliments me for being able to hold my own in any setting. We both enjoy theater, music and travel. He treasures the cultural benefits I bring him as a docent at our world class Philadelphia Museum Of Art. In addition, he feels very strongly as I do about giving back through volunteer work to help those less fortunate than we are. In addition to the art museum, I am involved with a wheelchair community and he serves in the recovery room of a major hospital.

Perhaps best of all, he is my upper when I am a downer. He listens to me and supports me when I'm in a sullen mood. At the same time, he urges me to understand that these are the years that count in our lives and we must bend every effort to get the most from them.

He holds to the belief that
sensitivity and affection should be
a life-long commitment and that
satisfying each other's needs is
the bottom line to any successful
marriage. Because, when you lose
the ability to do that, you have
entered a void from which there
is no return.

Let me not write the finish lines
to this book without mentioning
my good fortune in having a sister
who has been my steadfast friend
throughout life. She has nourished
me every step of the way with her
kind and gentle care-giving. I have

never known anyone more worthy of earthly rewards.

My tribute to her is to quote the poet Christina Georgina Rossetti who in the 1800s wrote:

> *. . . there is no friend like a sister*
> *In calm or stormy weather;*
> *To cheer one on the tedious way,*
> *To fetch one if one goes astray,*
> *To lift one if one totters down,*
> *To strengthen whilst one stands.*

Cristina Rossetti also had this advice on how to deal with life's inevitable setbacks and letdowns.

Better by far you forget and smile
Than that you should remember
and be sad.

Many are the blessings that make my life different this time around. Many were missing the first time around.

So, maybe after all, the hurt doesn't have to last for . . . a lifetime.

NOTES

NOTES

www.ingramcontent.com/pod-product-compliance
Lightning Source LLC
Chambersburg PA
CBHW031239280526
45784CB00004B/1642